WATCH OUT!

On the Road

Honor Head

WAYLAND

Explore the world with **Popcorn** - your complete first non-fiction library.

Look out for more titles in the **Popcorn** range. All books have the same format of simple text and striking images. Text is carefully matched to the pictures to help readers to identify and understand key vocabulary.
www.waylandbooks.co.uk/popcorn

First published in 2009 by Wayland

Copyright © Wayland 2009

Wayland
338 Euston Road
London NW1 3BH

Wayland Australia
Level 17/207 Kent Street
Sydney NSW 2000

Editor: Jean Coppendale
Designer: Alix Wood
Picture research: Taglines Creative Limited

British Library Cataloguing in Publication Data:
Head, Honor
    On the road. - (Popcorn. Watch out!)
    1. Traffic safety - Juvenile literature
    I. Title II. Series III. By road
    363.1'25-dc22

ISBN 978 0 7502 5792 3

Printed and bound in China

Wayland is a division of Hachette Children's Books,
an Hachette UK Company.
www.hachette.co.uk

Photographs:
Cover, 10, Photo and Co/Getty; 4 Paul Souders/Corbis; 5, 6, 7, 8, 9, 13 Crazy Quilt Bouquet; 11 By Ian Miles-Flashpoint Pictures/Alamy; 12 Jeff Dalton/Shutterstock; 14 MasPix/Alamy; 15 EML/Shutterstock; 16 Greenland/Shutterstock; 17 Ashley Jouhar/Getty; 18 Radius Images/Alamy; 19 Chris Howes/WildPlaces Photography/Alamy; 20; Markus Moellenberg/zefa/Corbis; 21 Sonya Etchison/Shutterstock

Contents

Be street smart

Busy roads have lots of traffic, such as cars, buses, motorbikes, vans and lorries.

What different types of traffic can you see in this picture?

When you are out, look and listen to what is happening around you. Cross the road at a proper crossing point.

Always look and listen before you cross the road.

⬤ Walking

When you are walking beside a road, walk on the pavement. Try to walk on the side of the pavement furthest from the cars.

Never cross the road between parked cars or near a corner. You might not see the cars coming.

Hold hands with your Mum or Dad when you are near traffic.

If you want to cross the road, look for a safe place. Use a footbridge or a subway if there is one.

Use a footbridge to cross a busy main road.

The Green Cross Code

The Green Cross Code will help you to cross the road safely. Follow these three steps.

1. Find a safe place to cross, such as a zebra crossing, traffic lights, a school crossing, an island or a clear stretch of road.

2. Stand on the pavement and look both ways along the road. Listen carefully. If you hear a car coming, wait until it has passed.

3. Only cross the road when you cannot see or hear any traffic coming from either direction. Walk quickly across the road without stopping but do not run.

Zebra crossings

At a zebra crossing cars have to stop and let you cross. Wait on the pavement until the traffic stops for you. Look both ways, then cross on the black and white stripes.

Walk across a zebra crossing, do not run.

Sometimes there is an island in the middle of the road. Use the Green Cross Code to cross to the island. Wait, and then use the Green Cross Code to cross to the pavement on the other side.

School time

Many schools have a special place to cross.
Wait on the pavement for the school
crossing patrol to stop the traffic
and then cross the road.

When it is safe
to cross, walk
across the road,
do not run.

Patrol

At a bus stop, wait on the pavement.
Let people get off the bus before
you get on.

Wait for the bus to move away from
the bus stop before you cross the road.

Pedestrian crossing

Most busy streets have a pedestrian crossing.
This is a safe place to cross the road. Push
the button at the traffic lights and wait.

Only cross the road when you see the green man light up and all the traffic has stopped.

Do not cross until you see the green man, even if there are no cars in sight.

Most traffic lights make a beeping noise to tell you when it is safe to cross.

On your bike

Riding a bike is great exercise, but do not ride on the pavement or on a busy road. Enjoy a bike ride in the local park or a place where there are no cars.

helmet

knee pads

It is important to wear safety clothing when you ride your bike.

If you are cycling when it is getting dark, make sure the lights on your bike work. Wear reflective clothing that shines in the dark so people can see you.

This boy's yellow jacket will shine when it gets dark.

Always make sure your bike is locked up safely if you have to leave it somewhere.

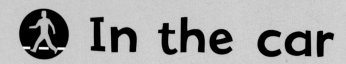 In the car

In a car, sit in a booster seat and wear a seat belt. Never shout at the driver or make the driver look away from the road.

Get in and out of a car on the pavement side only.

Keep your hands and head inside the car at all times, even when it is not moving. Never dangle things out of the window or throw anything onto the road.

If you get stuck in a traffic jam, stay inside the car.

Country roads

Many country roads do not have a pavement so you may have to walk in the road. If there is no pavement, walk so that you are facing the traffic.

When you are walking your dog always keep it on a lead. If you are near a busy road keep your dog away from the traffic.

Make sure your dog is properly trained before walking it near the road.

What's safe and what's not?

Try these road safety puzzles. Answers on page 24.

1. Which pictures below show
   a safe place to cross the road?

2. Think of what order these pictures should
   be in to show the Green Cross Code.

Glossary

booster seat a safety seat that a child sits on in the car so that the safety belt fits properly

footbridge a bridge people use to cross a busy road

island a place in the middle of a wide road where you can stop to wait for traffic to pass

reflective clothing special clothing that shines in the dark so that people can see you

safety clothing helmets and knee pads that stop you getting hurt if you fall off your bike

subway a tunnel that goes from one side of a busy road to the other

Index

Answers to puzzles: 1. a and c. 2. a, c, b